IMAGES FROM THE BIBLE

A Celebration

IMAGES
FROM THE
BIBLE

A Celebration

HUNT&
THORPE

THE CREATION

⟨⟩

 HIS FRESCO is an artistic interpretation of the first five "days" of creation, based on Genesis chapter one. Day one gave light. Day two gave the sky and day three the land, with its trees and vegetation. Day four gave the sun and moon. The waters are to teem with life and the birds fly over the earth on day five. The creation springs from the Creator God, who stands there, hand raised in blessing.

In the beginning God created the heavens and the earth.
God said, "Let there be light, and there was light ... – the
first day. God saw all that he made, and it was very good.
And God said, "Let the water teem with living creatures,
and let birds fly above the earth across the expanse of the
sky" ... – the fifth day.

GENESIS 1:1,3,20,23

CREATION OF THE ANIMALS
*Sucevita Monastery, Romania,
16th century*

EVE

~

ALBRECHT DÜRER'S portrayal of the fall of mankind focuses on the beautiful, innocent-looking, attractive full-length painting of the naked Eve. In stark contrast to this fetching exterior are her inner thoughts. The serpent has beguiled her. She takes the apple, tastes it for herself, and then gives it to Adam, encouraging him, too, to disobey God and eat the forbidden fruit. The lure of temptation wins.

Now the serpent was more crafty than any of the wild animals the Lord God had made. He said to the woman, "Did God really say, 'You must not eat from any tree in the garden?'"… When the woman saw that the fruit of the tree was good for food and pleasing to the eye, and also desirable for gaining wisdom, she took some and ate it. She also gave some to her husband, who was with her, and he ate it.

GENESIS 3:1,6

GERMAN EVE
Albrecht Dürer, 1471–1528

7

Noah's Ark

~

$\mathcal{N}$OAH'S ARK, and boats in general, represent God's deliverance and safety. The ark is almost in the shape of a church building – as God's salvation was so linked to the church. All the animals and birds will find their security in the ark. The foreground figures are treading grapes for wine and becoming drunk – scoffing at Noah building a huge boat on dry land, hundreds of miles from any sea.

> *God said to Noah, "I am going to put an end to all people,*
> *for the earth is filled with violence because of them … So*
> *make yourself an ark of cypress wood; make rooms in it and*
> *coat it with pitch inside and out … You are to enter the ark*
> *– you and your sons and your wife and your sons' wives*
> *with you. You are to bring into the ark two of all*
> *living creatures."*
>
> GENESIS 6:13,14,18,19

BUILDING NOAH'S ARK
Bedford Book of Hours, c. 1423

THE TOWER OF BABEL

THE TOWER OF BABEL symbolized mankind's pride and arrogance. The people of Babel set about building a tower that would reach the heavens. They were determined to make a name for themselves through their building programme, which is reflected in the magnificence of the tower in this painting. This did not meet with God's pleasure, as is seen from the figures being thrown off the top of the tower by some flying "heavenly" beings.

> *They said, "Come let us build ourselves a city, with a tower that reaches to the heavens, so that we may make a name for ourselves"… But the Lord came down to the city and the tower… and said, "Come let us go down and confuse their language so they will not understand each other."*
>
> GENESIS 11:4,5,7

BUILDING THE TOWER OF BABEL
Bedford Book of Hours, c. 1423

MOSES

⁓

MOSES STANDS on dry land with tens of thousands of Israelites behind him, who had just fled from their slavery in Egypt. The Red Sea had been a wall of water to them on their right and on their left. And Pharaoh had sent his six hundred best chariots and soldiers to bring them back. This painting captures the moment when "Moses stretched out his hand over the sea" so that the water covered the chariots and soldiers. The Exodus was complete.

Moses stretched out his hand over the sea, and at daybreak the sea went back to its place. The Egyptians were fleeing and the Lord swept them into the sea. The water flowed back and covered the chariots and horsemen – the entire army of Pharaoh that had followed the Israelites into the sea. Not one of them survived.

EXODUS 14:7–28

AND MOSES STRETCHED FORTH
HIS HAND OVER THE SEA
Ivan Konstantinovich Aivazovsky, 1817–1900

DAVID AND GOLIATH

❧

$\mathcal{T}$HE ARTIST gives a very idealized picture of David. In real life David was a strong teenage shepherd. In this painting he has delicate hands and is dressed in fine silks and satins, complete with a hat which was doubtless most fashionable in the seventeenth century. Clearly, the artist is telling us that David's victory over the Philistine champion, Goliath, was effortless, as he touches the giant's head, which he has just beheaded with the giant's own sword, which he still holds.

David said to the Philistine, "You come against me with sword and spear and javelin, but I come against you in the name of the Lord Almighty, the God of the armies of Israel, whom you have defied. This day the Lord will hand you over to me, and I'll strike you down and cut off your head." … Reaching into his bag and taking out a stone, David slung it and struck the Philistine on the forehead… So David triumphed over the Philistine with a sling and a stone.

1 SAMUEL 17:45,46,49,50

DAVID WITH HEAD OF GOLIATH
Carlo Dolci, 1616–1686

THE QUEEN OF SHEBA

⌒

$\mathcal{T}$HIS PORTRAYAL of the Queen of Sheba visiting and kneeling before the wise and wealthy King Solomon is full of many of the trappings of fifteenth-century culture. The buildings in the background, Solomon's throne, and the dresses all reflect fifteenth-century Europe. However, the splendor and regal setting depicted in the painting capture the atmosphere that must have been present in King Solomon's magnificent court.

> *When the queen of Sheba heard about the fame of Solomon and his relation to the name of the Lord, she came to test him with hard questions … When the queen of Sheba saw all the wisdom of Solomon and the palace he had built, the food on his table, the seating of his officials, the attending servants in their robes, the cupbearers, and the burnt offerings he made at the temple of the Lord, she was overcome.*

1 KINGS 10:1,4–5

THE QUEEN OF SHEBA
KNEELS BEFORE KING SOLOMON
Grimani breviary, att. Hans Memling,
15th century

ESTHER

THE TWO THINGS Esther is famous for are emphasized in this painting. She was a beauty queen, and had to win a beauty contest to become King Xerxes' replacement wife. Her natural beauty shines through all the jewellery and finery she had to wear as queen of the world's greatest superpower. Esther's secret was that she was a Jewess, and so was able to save the Jewish people from what seemed to be a certain holocaust. Hence the significance and prominence of the Jewish, seven-branched candlestick, *menorah*, in this painting.

> *Let a search be made for beautiful young virgins for the king… Now the king was attracted to Esther more than to any of the other women… So he set a royal crown on her head and made her queen instead of Vashti.*
>
> *Esther pleaded with the king, falling at his feet and weeping. She begged him to put an end to the evil plan of Haman the Agagite, which he had devised against the Jews. Then the king extended the gold sceptre to Esther and she arose and stood before him… [So] the Jews got relief from their enemies.*
>
> ESTHER 2:2,17; 8:3,4; 9:22

ESTHER
Edouard Richter, 1844–1913

BETHLEHEM

❧

𝒯HIS MOST UNUSUAL depiction of the visit of the Magi has an angel holding the star that led the three wise men to the birth of a new king, whom these astrologers were seeking. The wise men, with heads reverently bowed, each have a gift for the baby Jesus: gold, frankincense, and myrrh. The subdued colors, surrounding country scenery, growing flowers, and the simple structure Mary sits under all add to the ethereal atmosphere of Burne-Jones' painting.

> *After Jesus was born in Bethlehem in Judea, during the time of King Herod, Magi from the east came to Jerusalem, and asked, "Where is the one who has been born king of the Jews? We saw his star in the east and have to worship him." ... The star they had seen in the east went ahead of them until it stopped over the place where the child was. When they saw the star they were overjoyed. On coming to the house they saw the child with his mother Mary and they bowed down and worshipped him. They opened their treasures and presented him with gifts of gold and of incense and of myrrh.*
>
> MATTHEW 2:1–2, 9–11

THE STAR OF BETHLEHEM
Edward Coley Burne-Jones, 1833–1898

ST. JOHN THE BAPTIST

⌒

THE AUTHENTIC John the Baptist lies beneath the gorgeous green cape, which signified the esteem in which the martyred St. John the Baptist was held by the Church. The camel's hair shirt, and bare feet, are emblems of his Old Testament-style prophetic ministry. His thunderous preaching about repenting of sins is symbolized by the book (a Bible) that he holds. His hand is raised in blessing, reminding us of his ministry of baptism in the River Jordan, especially his baptism of Jesus.

> *In those days John the Baptist came, preaching in the Desert of Judea and saying, "Repent, for the kingdom of heaven is near."… John's clothes were made of camel's hair, and he had a leather belt round his waist. His food was locusts and wild honey. People went out to him from Jerusalem and all Judea and the whole region of the Jordan. Confessing their sins, they were baptized by him in the Jordan River.*
>
> MATTHEW 3:1–2, 9–11

ST. JOHN THE BAPTIST
Hubert & Jan Van Eyck, c. 1400

THE WOMAN OF SAMARIA

∼

$\mathcal{T}$HE SEATED FIGURE is Christ, who is resting on a journey as the noon-day sun beats down. A local woman from nearby Samaria arrives at Jacob's well, which also has two large wooden drinking troughs for animals. Jesus asks her for a drink of water to quench his physical thirst, as a prelude to telling her about the spiritual water he could give her – "a well of water welling up to eternal life." The other figures are the twelve apostles, who were amazed to find Christ deigning to speak to a woman in public – and a despised half-caste Samaritan at that.

> *Now Jesus had to go through Samaria… Jacob's well was there, and Jesus, tired as he was from the journey, sat down at the well. It was about the sixth hour. When a Samaritan woman came to draw water, Jesus said to her, "Will you give me a drink?"… Jesus said, "Everyone who drinks this water will be thirsty again, but whoever drinks the water I give him will never thirst. Indeed, the water I give him will become in him a spring of water welling up to eternal life."*
>
> JOHN 4:4,6,7,13

CHRIST AND THE WOMAN OF SAMARIA
Karl Marko, 1791–1860

THE ASCENSION

CHRIST is depicted as ascending from a small mount on earth to a vast heavenly sky. His eleven apostles kneel, in addition to the separate kneeling figure of a woman, Mary, the mother of Jesus, all worshipping the ascending Christ. Christ is greeted in heaven by countless angels. The two angels below Christ have a special message for Christ's followers, which they are in the middle of delivering.

> *They were looking intently up into the sky as he was going, when suddenly two men dressed in white stood beside them. "Men of Galilee," they said, "why do you stand here looking into the sky? This same Jesus, who has been taken from you into heaven, will come back in the same way you have seen him go into heaven."*

ACTS 1:10–11

THE ASCENSION OF CHRIST
Giotto di Bondone, 1276–1337

The Last Judgement

❧

$\mathcal{T}$HIS PICTURE of the last judgement is crammed full of numerous examples of symbolism. Christ, seated in glory in the heavens, gives his sword of judgement to his apostles to carry out the divine judgement, while two angels blow on their golden trumpets. The great confusion and mass of detail on earth are resolved when it is seen that those on Christ's left-hand side are all images of the damned destined for hell, and those on Christ's right-hand side are the righteous and redeemed destined for heaven.

> *When the Son of Man comes in his glory, and all the angels with him, he will sit on his throne in heavenly glory. All the nations will be gathered before him, and he will separate the people one from another as a shepherd separates the sheep from the goats. He will put the sheep on his right and the goats on his left.*
>
> MATTHEW 25:31–33

THE LAST JUDGEMENT
Hieronymus Bosch, 1450–1516

BABYLON

THE WINGED ANGEL blows his horn, to announce some very important news, and spreads light all around. Blood-red flames of fire graphically illustrate the destruction of Babylon. The figure and heads of bodies at the bottom of the painting represent the innumerable Christian martyrs that have been killed by godless people – Babylon – throughout the ages. But now, at last, Babylon is herself under divine judgement.

After this I saw another angel coming down from heaven.
He had great authority, and the earth was illuminated by
his splendour. With a mighty voice he shouted:
  "Fallen! Fallen is Babylon the Great!"
  ... In her was found the blood of prophets and of saints.
REVELATION 18:1–2,24

THE FALL OF THE CITY OF BABYLON
*Liebana Beautus commentary on
the Apocalypse from Guadalupe,
10th century*

Originally published by HUNT & THORPE 1996
Designed by THE BRIDGEWATER BOOK COMPANY LIMITED

ISBN 1 85608 249 0

In Australia this book is published by:
HUNT & THORPE Australia Pty Ltd.
9 Euston Street, Rydalmere NSW 2116

Write to:
HUNT & THORPE
Laurel House, Station Approach
New Alresford, Hants SO24 9JH

A CIP catalogue record for this book is available from the
British Library.

Printed and bound in Singapore.

The publishers wish to thank the following for the use of pictures:
E.T. ARCHIVE: p.17; Biblioteca dell' Escorial, Spain half title and
p.31; Brera, Milan p.15; British Library pp.9, 11; Prado, Madrid
cover, title page and p.7; Scroregni Chapel, Padua p.27; Sucevita
Monastery, Moldovia p.5; Suermondt Museum, Aachen p.29;
FINE ART PHOTOGRAPHIC LIBRARY: pp.13, 19, 21, 23, 25.

Cover illustration
The Immaculate Conception, Bartolome Esteban Murillo, 1618-82